Designed by Nature

Energy Technology

James Bow
and John Willis

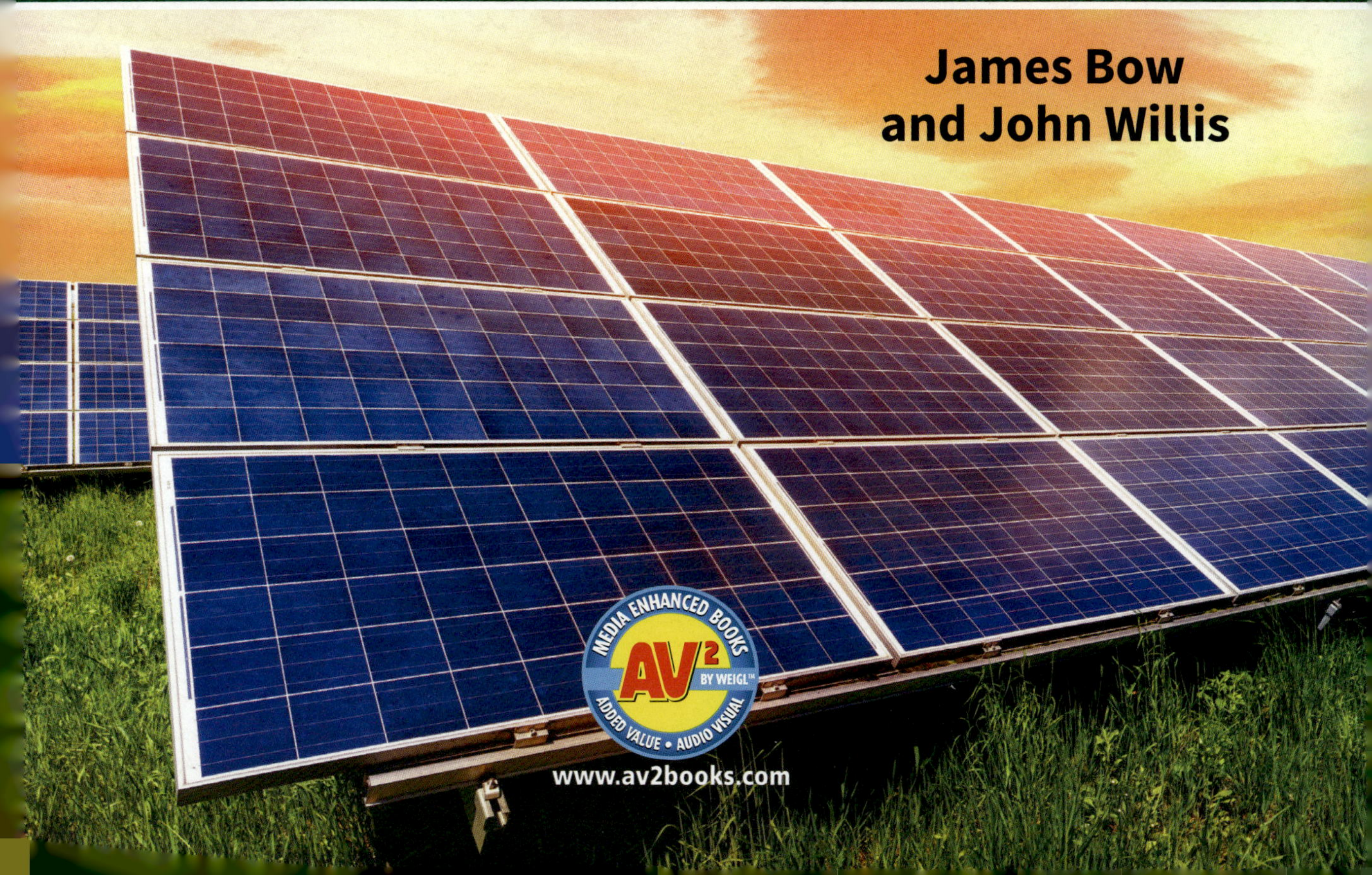

www.av2books.com

AV² provides enriched content that supplements and complements this book. Weigl's AV² books strive to create inspired learning and engage young minds in a total learning experience.

Your AV² Media Enhanced books come alive with...

Audio
Listen to sections of the book read aloud.

Video
Watch informative video clips.

Embedded Weblinks
Gain additional information for research.

Try This!
Complete activities and hands-on experiments.

Key Words
Study vocabulary, and complete a matching word activity.

Quizzes
Test your knowledge.

Slide Show
View images and captions, and prepare a presentation.

... and much, much more!

Go to www.av2books.com, and enter this book's unique code.

BOOK CODE

AVG28928

AV² by Weigl brings you media enhanced books that support active learning.

Published by AV² by Weigl
350 5th Avenue, 59th Floor
New York, NY 10118
Website: www.av2books.com

Library of Congress Cataloging-in-Publication Data available upon request.
Fax 1-866-44-WEIGL for the attention of the Publishing Records department.

ISBN 978-1-4896-9721-9 (hardcover)
ISBN 978-1-4896-9722-6 (softcover)
ISBN 978-1-4896-9723-3 (multi-user eBook)
ISBN 978-1-4896-9724-0 (single-user eBook)

Printed in the United States of America in Brainerd, Minnesota
1 2 3 4 5 6 7 8 9 0 22 21 20 19 18

122018
102318

Project Coordinator: John Willis   Designer: Ana María Vidal

Every reasonable effort has been made to trace ownership and to obtain permission to reprint copyright material. The publishers would be pleased to have any errors or omissions brought to their attention so that they may be corrected in subsequent printings.

Weigl acknowledges Alamy, Getty Images, iStock, Newscom, Shutterstock, and Wikimedia as its primary image suppliers for this title.

First published by North Star Editions in 2019

Designed by Nature

Contents

Chapter 1

Chlorophyll, in plant leaves, gives them a green color.

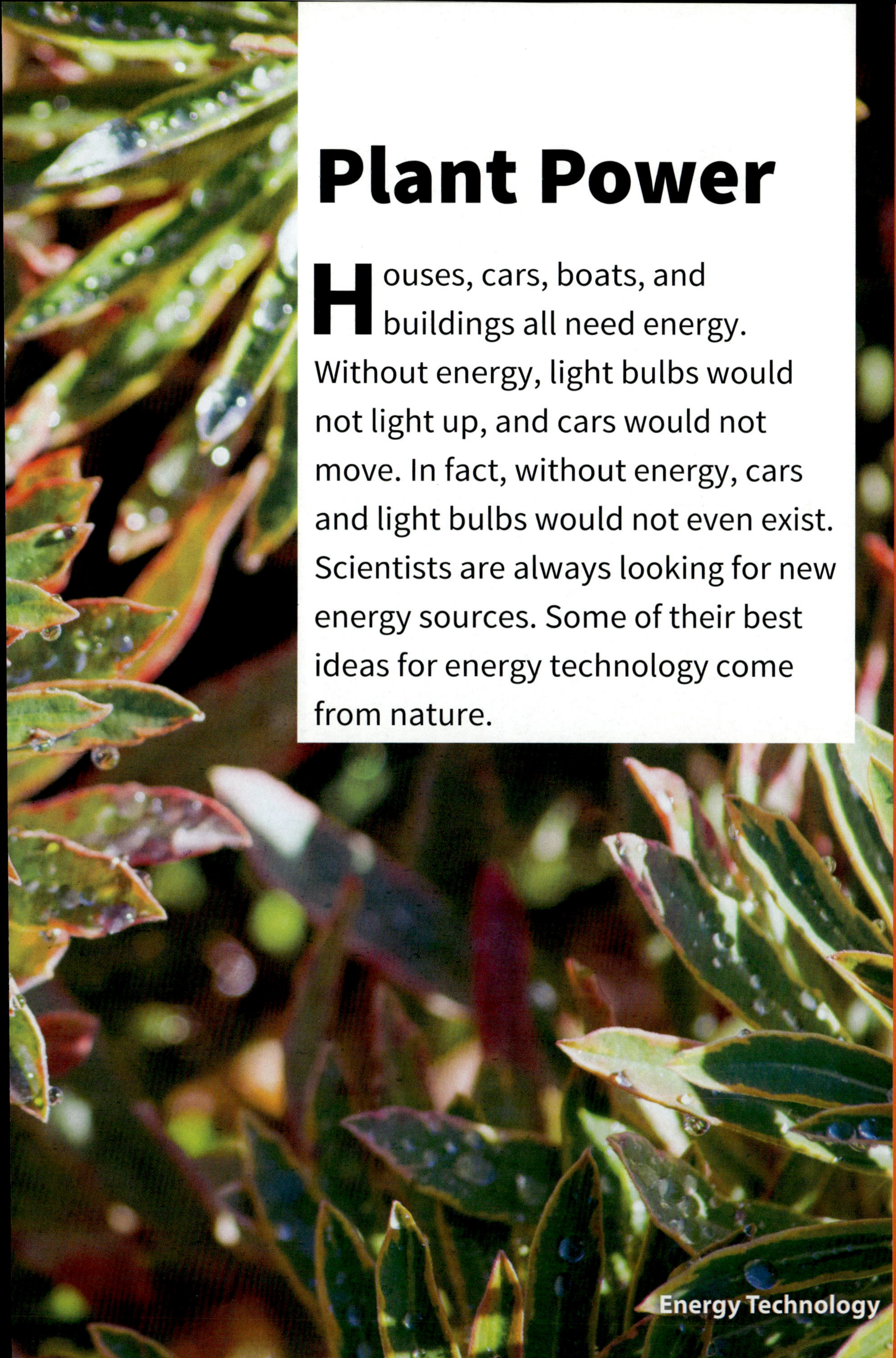

Plant Power

Houses, cars, boats, and buildings all need energy. Without energy, light bulbs would not light up, and cars would not move. In fact, without energy, cars and light bulbs would not even exist. Scientists are always looking for new energy sources. Some of their best ideas for energy technology come from nature.

Mimicking nature to solve human problems is called biomimicry. Plants create the energy they need through **photosynthesis**. In this process, plants absorb **solar** energy through their leaves. They turn energy from the Sun into energy they can store for later.

The PS10 solar plant in Seville, Spain, uses 624 mirrors to light a 40-story tower.

Solar panels use a slightly different process. These devices turn sunlight into electricity. Scientists have improved solar panels by studying sunflowers. Sunflowers turn to face the Sun during the day. This helps them gather as much energy as possible.

How Solar Panels Work

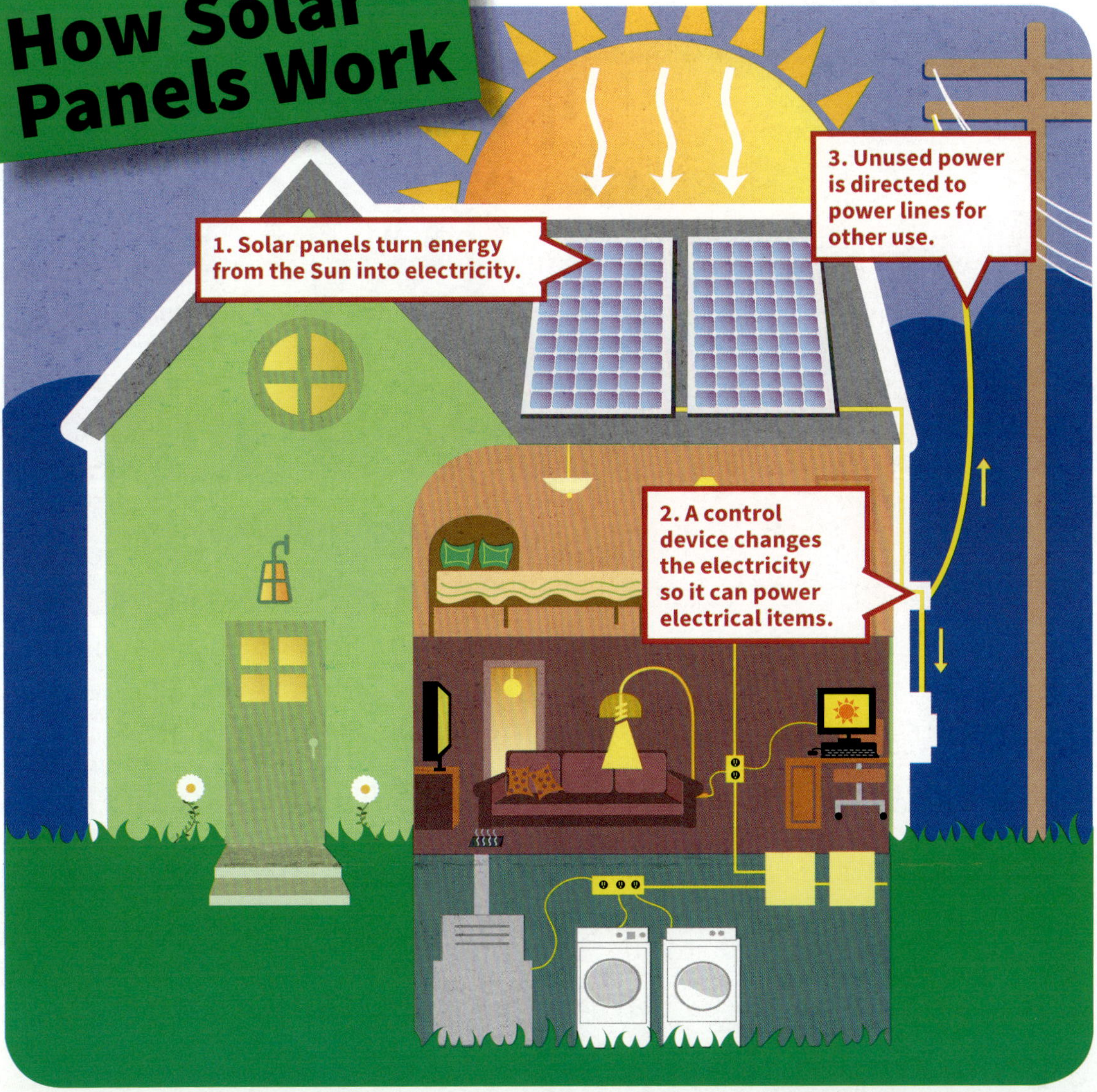

Inspired by Trees

Windmills turn energy from wind into another form of energy. Scientists have worked to improve windmills by studying trees. They found that branches help trees catch wind. This gave scientists an idea. Most windmills have one large **generator**. But the scientists created a windmill that has many generators. This new windmill has branches, similar to a tree. At the end of each branch is a small generator. Scientists set up the first "tree" windmills in Paris, France, in 2016.

Scientists used a similar method to create a solar **power plant**. They built clusters of mirrors around a central tower. The mirrors reflect the Sun's energy at the tower. Then, the tower turns the energy into electricity. Similar to sunflowers, the mirrors turn as the Sun crosses the sky.

These mirrors do not face the Sun directly. Instead, the mirrors find an angle that reflects the most energy at the tower.

Humans often create electricity by burning coal and oil. However, these energy sources are not **renewable**. They will eventually run out. Burning coal and oil also releases carbon dioxide into Earth's atmosphere. This process is harmful to the planet. Scientists hope solar power can replace other energy sources.

The first photosynthetic bacteria formed more than **3 billion years ago**.

People first began studying photosynthesis in **1771**.

Sugar cane is one of the plants **most efficient** at photosynthesis.

Chapter 2

A humpback whale's front flippers are about 15 feet long. (4.6 meters)

Animal Power

Many animals have **adapted** to their environments. Their bodies may have features that help them move. For example, whales and dolphins have long, narrow bodies. This shape helps them swim quickly. Some scientists study animals to improve energy technology. They look for ways to produce more power with less effort.

Wind is a major source of renewable energy. But windmills can produce power only when there is a certain amount of wind. Scientists wanted windmills to produce more power. They turned to the humpback whale for answers.

The wind energy industry in the United States grew by 9 percent in 2017.

The average humpback weighs more than 80,000 pounds (36,000 kilograms). It can swim up to 17 miles per hour (27 kilometers per hour). Scientists wondered how an animal so big could move so fast. They studied the ridges on the front edge of the humpback's fins.

Mimicking the Sea Sponge

Solar panels are made of an element called silicon. Companies carve and melt silicon to make panels. These methods use large amounts of energy. The sea sponge, a type of sea animal, may have a better idea. Sea sponges create silicon from seawater. They shape the silicon to build their bodies. Scientists hope to mimic how sea sponges grow. The goal is to make silicon form itself into solar panels. This would require less energy than current methods.

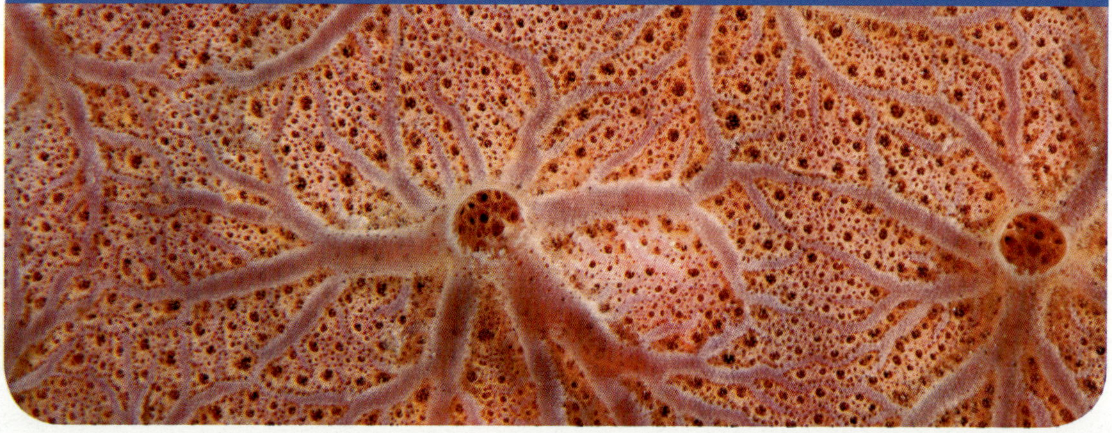

Birds in a v-formation time their wing flaps to use upward-moving air made by birds in front of them.

These ridges are called **tubercles**. They help the whale cut through water more easily. Scientists added similar ridges to windmill blades. These new windmills can move through the air more easily. That means they make more energy from less wind.

Animals also work together to save energy. For example, geese fly in groups. They form the shape of a V. The goose in front uses the most energy. As the goose flies, it pushes air upward at the tips of its wings. This upward-moving air helps lift the other geese. As a result, they need less energy to fly.

Fish also move together to save energy. Some schools of fish swim in a diamond shape. Scientists placed windmills in a similar diamond-shaped pattern. The windmill in front created a movement of air. The windmills in back used the movement of air to spin more easily. This helped the windmills make more energy.

Chapter 3

Coal-powered plants are harmful to the environment.

Saving Energy

Many energy sources are not renewable. They use up important resources such as oil. They also pollute the air. Humans can protect Earth by using less energy. This is called conservation. Scientists are searching for new ways to conserve energy. They often find solutions in nature.

The firefly has a light organ on its abdomen.

Fireflies produce a cold light. They waste little energy in the form of heat. To create the light, chemicals react inside the firefly's body. Scientists tried to copy this chemical reaction. But they could not make as much light as the firefly. They studied the firefly closer. They saw that it had small, overlapping scales. The scales help the firefly's light escape outward. This makes the light brighter.

In 2013, scientists applied a similar pattern to light bulbs. They used LEDs, or light-emitting diodes. LEDs use less energy than typical bulbs. The pattern made the LEDs 55 percent brighter. The bulbs used less energy to light a room.

Lighting a city is an even greater task. Cities use large power plants to create electricity. One power plant provides electricity to many buildings. However, the electricity must travel far to reach the buildings. As electricity travels, it loses energy in the form of heat. Scientists are looking for other ways to provide power.

Bees may hold the solution. In a beehive, each bee has a small task. But together, the bees build and maintain the hive. Scientists want to mimic this method to power homes and buildings. They would replace one large power plant with many small plants. Homes would have solar panels on the roof.

Shaped by Storms

Tornadoes and whirlpools move in circular patterns. The spiral is a common shape in nature. It allows moving air or water to use less energy to maintain flow. Scientists built fans in a similar circular shape. The fans were able to move air more easily. They used less energy to cool rooms.

The Tesla Powerwall battery stores energy from solar panels for home use.

The energy from the panels would be stored in batteries. Then, the batteries would power nearby homes. That way, the energy would not have to travel far. This could save energy on a large scale.

Inspire Me!

Insect Inspiration

Termites are skilled builders. They build large, complex mounds in deserts. Despite the hot sunlight, the mound stays cool. Scientists wondered how this was possible. They found cooler, muddy areas that the termites had built near the bottom of the mounds. Cool air enters the mound from these areas. Inside, warm air rises. It escapes through huge, chimney-like structures.

Termite mounds inspired the design of the Eastgate Centre in Harare, Zimbabwe. The shopping center has shady areas at its base. Inside, hot air rises into large open areas. Then, it escapes through vents in the roof. This design was a success. The Eastgate Centre uses 10 percent of the energy needed to cool similar-sized buildings.

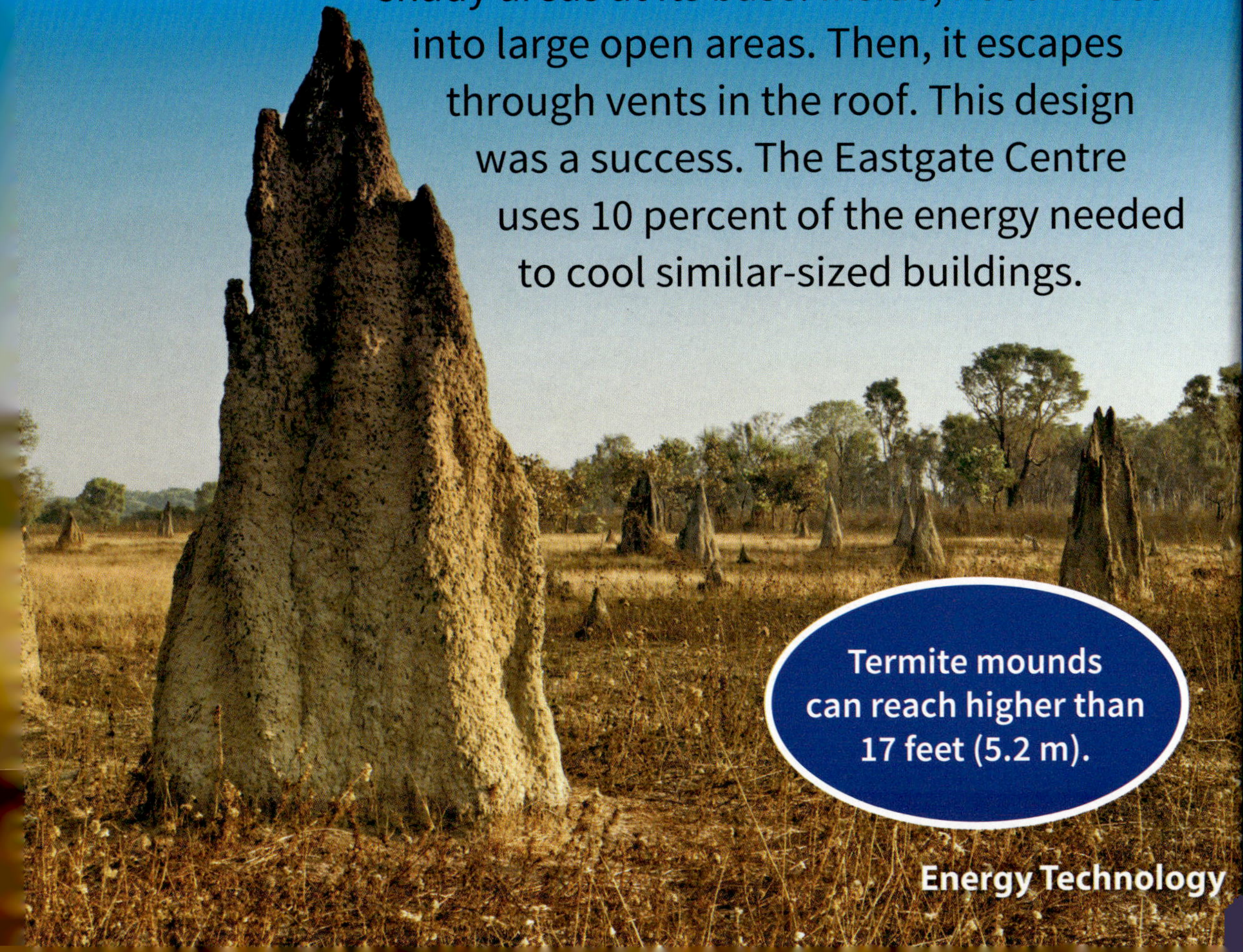

Termite mounds can reach higher than 17 feet (5.2 m).

Chapter 4

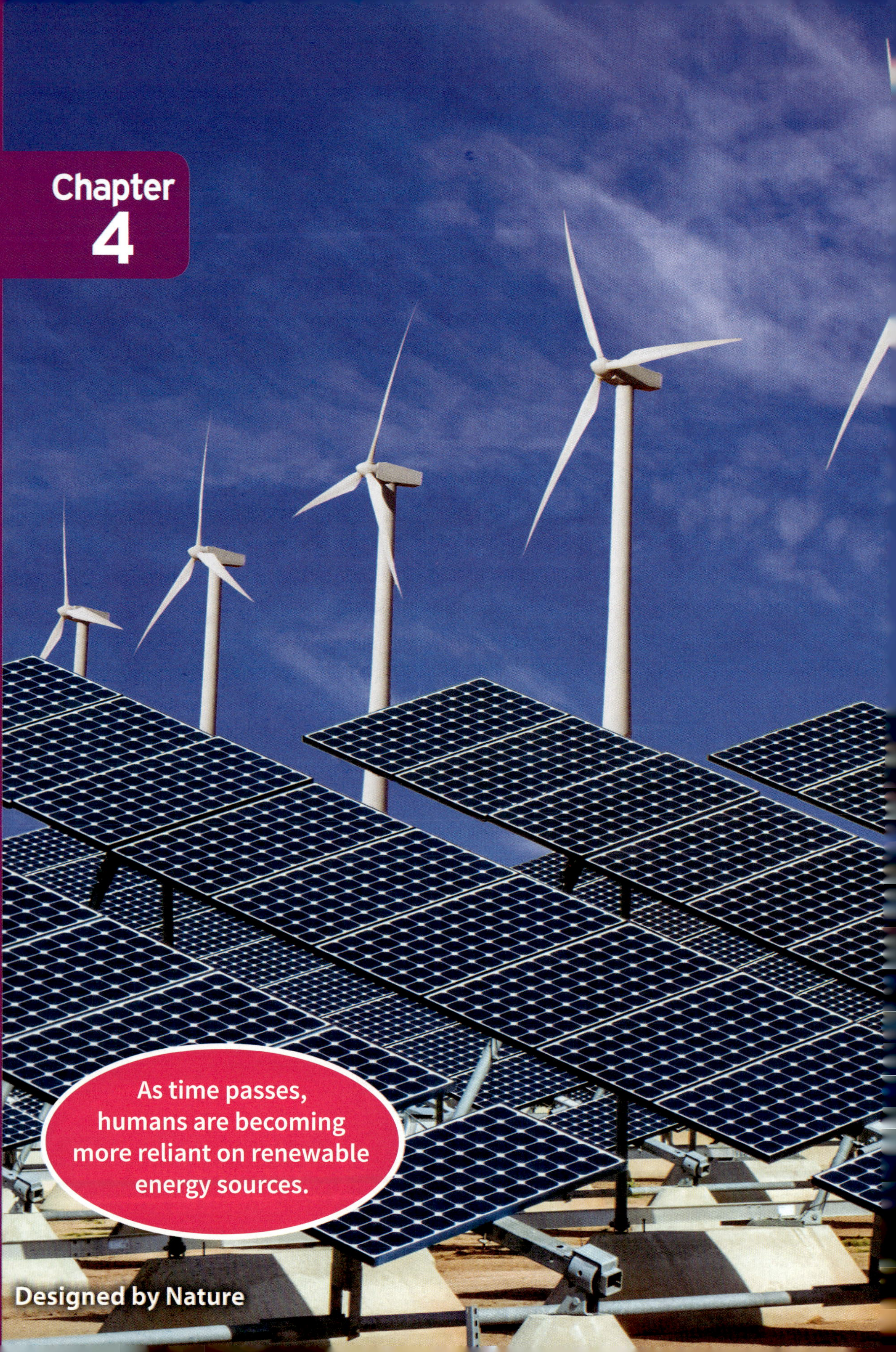

As time passes, humans are becoming more reliant on renewable energy sources.

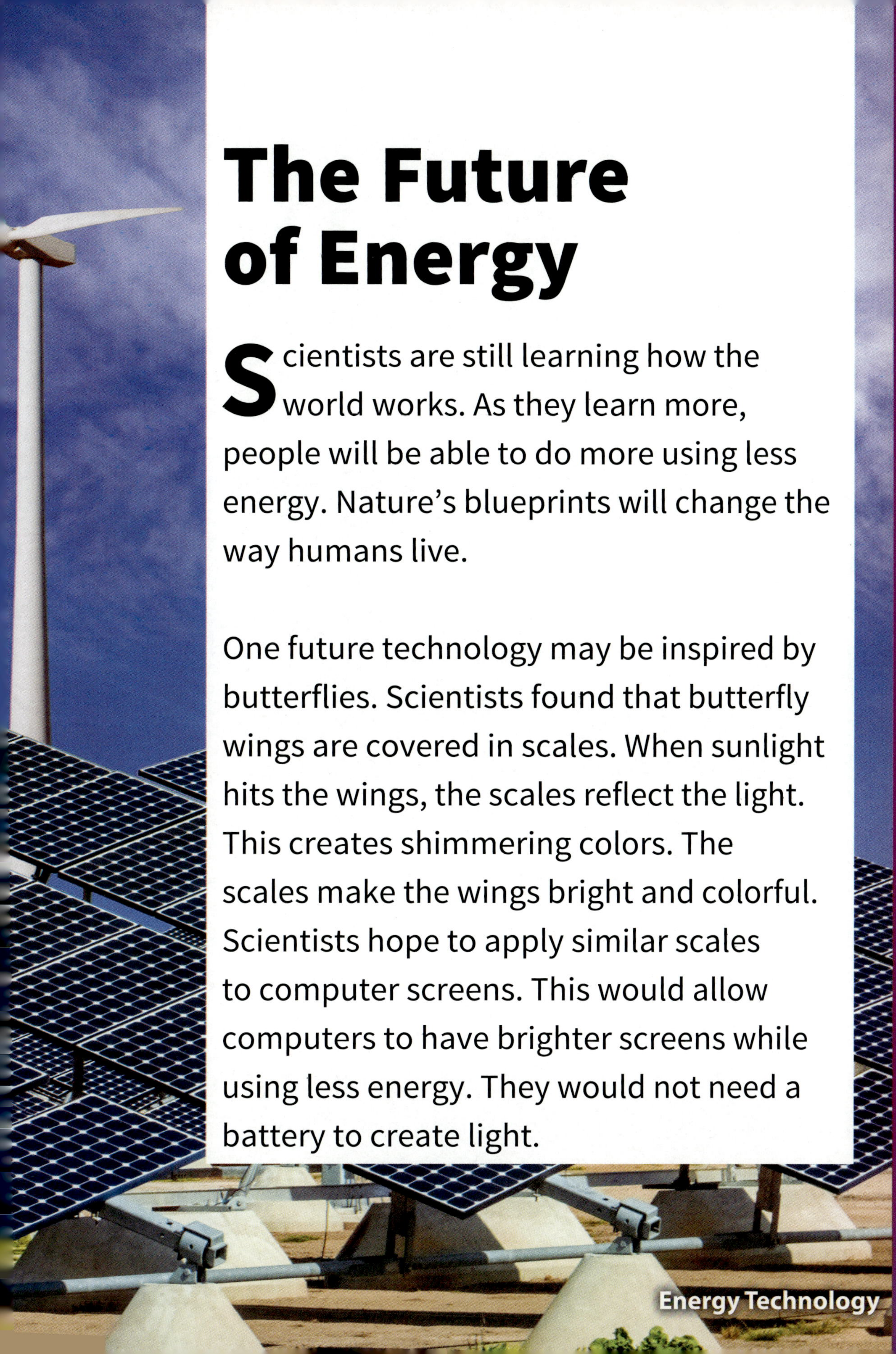

The Future of Energy

Scientists are still learning how the world works. As they learn more, people will be able to do more using less energy. Nature's blueprints will change the way humans live.

One future technology may be inspired by butterflies. Scientists found that butterfly wings are covered in scales. When sunlight hits the wings, the scales reflect the light. This creates shimmering colors. The scales make the wings bright and colorful. Scientists hope to apply similar scales to computer screens. This would allow computers to have brighter screens while using less energy. They would not need a battery to create light.

Alessandro Volta invented the first battery in about the year 1800.

Batteries are useful sources of energy. But some batteries are large and bulky. They can also die quickly. Scientists want to mimic plants to improve batteries. Plants take in energy from the Sun and store it as sugar. They use some of that sugar to create energy. This process inspired scientists to make batteries that are powered by sugar. These would be even lighter and more powerful than the batteries in cellphones.

One scientist is trying to mimic the power of tornadoes. First, the scientist sends hot air into a hollow tower. This creates a small whirlwind. Then, the energy from the whirlwind powers fans. The fans become generators, creating more energy. The scientist is still trying to make a larger whirlwind. If he does, he could create huge amounts of electricity.

In nature, the parts of an **ecosystem** work together. Plants turn sunlight into energy. Animals eat the plants. Then, the animals' waste helps other plants grow.

In **1938**, archaeologists discovered ancient battery-like objects that were more than **2,200 years old**.

Batteries were **first** sold in the United States in **1898**.

As of 2016, more than **2 million** battery-powered cars had been sold.

Many scientists think cities should act like ecosystems. Different parts of the city could work together to save energy. For example, one company in California uses waste from power plants to make cement. The waste contains carbon dioxide gas. The company turns the gas into **calcium carbonate**. This mineral is an ingredient in cement. Some sea animals also use a form of the mineral to build shells.

Usually, making cement requires large amounts of energy. But the California company saves energy by using another industry's waste. By following this company's example, ecosystem-inspired cities could grow using less energy.

Coral reefs are made up of layers of calcium carbonate.

Timeline

Humans have been using nature to inspire technology for thousands of years. As people understand nature more clearly, they are able to find new ways to create energy technology.

1996 Eastgate Centre opens in Harare, Zimbabwe. Based on a termite mound, it has 48 chimneys to allow hot air to escape.

2004 A skyscraper in London, England opens. Called 30 St Mary Axe, or "the gherkin," its sea-sponge-based design helps air flow throughout the building.

2006 BioPower Systems is founded in Australia. The company develops a wave energy generator using structures based on seaweed.

2013 Scales on fireflies are used as inspiration for more effective LEDs. Scientists copy the scales by using lasers to etch "factory roof" patterns on the lights.

2016 Researchers at Harvard University present a design for an "artificial leaf," that can be used to generate fuels.

2017 Researchers publish a study detailing a new device, based on an electric eel, that could be used to power implanted or worn electronics.

Energy Technology Map

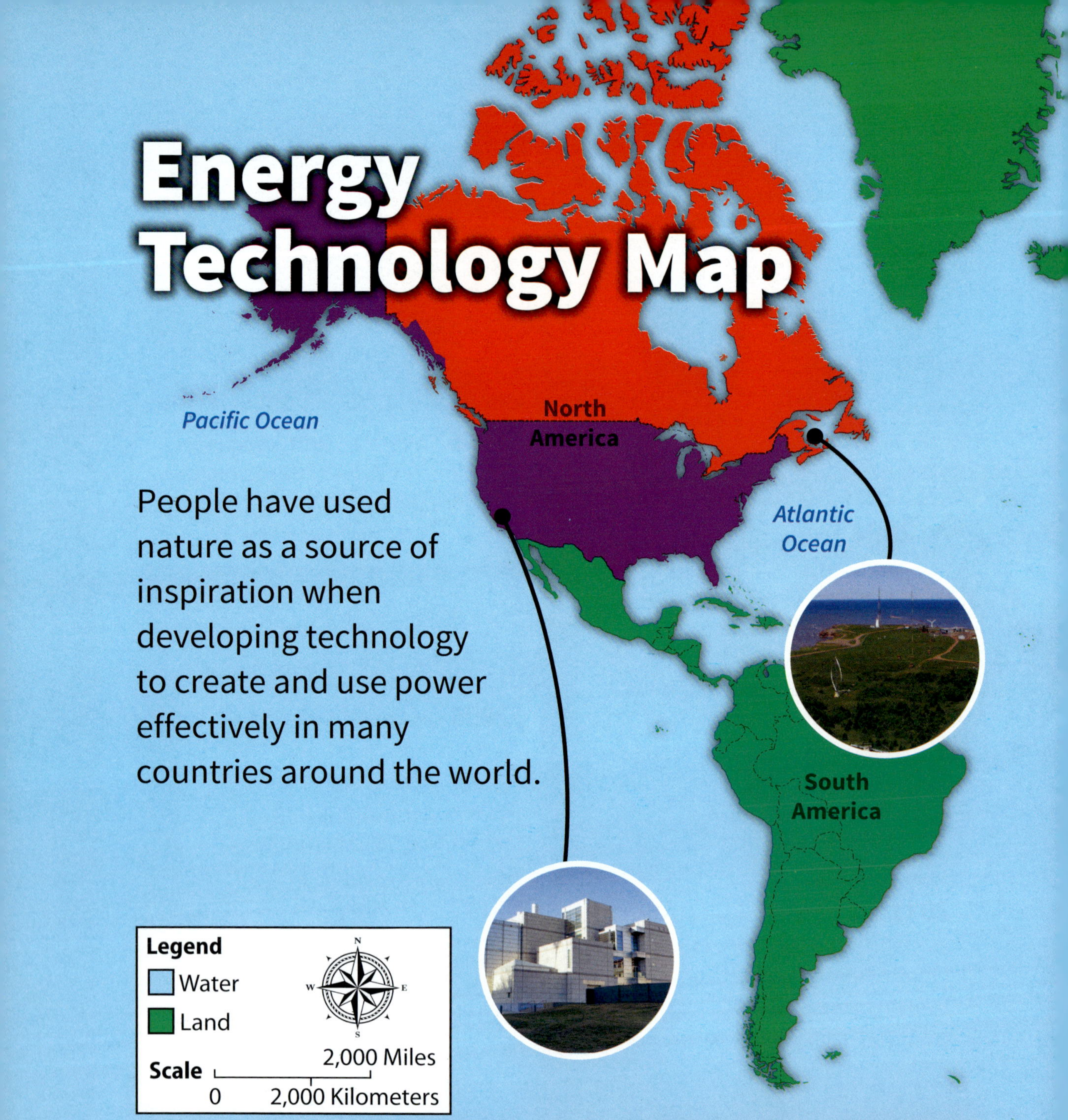

People have used nature as a source of inspiration when developing technology to create and use power effectively in many countries around the world.

United States

When John Dabiri was a professor at Caltech, he researched how wind farms could be structured like fish schools. He tested these windmills in California's desert.

Canada

Located on Prince Edward Island, the Wind Energy Institute of Canada has been the testing ground for many kinds of technology, including windmills based on whale tubercles.

France

"Wind Tree" windmills were first placed in the city of Paris, France, in 2015. Each tree, powered by leaf-like blades, is able to power 15 street lamps.

Zimbabwe

Eastgate Centre, in Harare, is one of the best-known buildings built using biomimicry. It is one of the first commercial buildings to rely entirely on passive cooling.

Quiz

1 What city received “Wind Tree” windmills in 2016?

Answer: Paris, France

2 When did people begin studying photosynthesis?

Answer: 1771

3 What gives plant leaves a green color?

Answer: Chlorophyll

4 When were batteries first sold in the United States?

Answer: 1898

5 Where is a firefly’s light organ?

Answer: On its abdomen

6 What is a tubercle?

Answer: A ridge on a humpback whale’s fin

7 When did the first photosynthetic bacteria form?

Answer: More than 3 billion years ago

8 What shape do flocks of geese form when they fly?

Answer: A “V” shape

9 How tall can a termite mound be?

Answer: Higher than 17 feet (5.2 m)

10 What mineral makes up coral reefs?

Answer: Calcium carbonate

Key Words

adapted: changed over time to deal with a certain situation

calcium carbonate: a solid substance found in nature as chalk, limestone, and marble

ecosystem: the collection of living things in a natural area

generator: a machine that produces electricity

mimicking: copying an appearance or behavior

photosynthesis: the process in which plants turn sunlight, carbon dioxide, and water into oxygen and energy

power plant: a place that generates electricity

renewable: having to do with natural resources that never run out

solar: having to do with the Sun

tubercles: knobby lumps on living things

Index

Log on to www.av2books.com

AV² by Weigl brings you media enhanced books that support active learning. Go to www.av2books.com, and enter the special code found on page 2 of this book. You will gain access to enriched and enhanced content that supplements and complements this book. Content includes video, audio, weblinks, quizzes, a slide show, and activities.

AV² Online Navigation

Audio
Listen to sections of the book read aloud.

Book Pages
AV² pages directly correspond to pages in the book.

Video
Watch informative video clips.

Embedded Weblinks
Gain additional information for research.

Key Words
Study vocabulary, and complete a matching word activity.

Try This!
Complete activities and hands-on experiments.

Quizzes
Test your knowledge.

Slide Show
View images and captions, and prepare a presentation.

AV² was built to bridge the gap between print and digital. We encourage you to tell us what you like and what you want to see in the future.

Sign up to be an AV² Ambassador at www.av2books.com/ambassador.

Due to the dynamic nature of the Internet, some of the URLs and activities provided as part of AV² by Weigl may have changed or ceased to exist. AV² by Weigl accepts no responsibility for any such changes. All media enhanced books are regularly monitored to update addresses and sites in a timely manner. Contact AV² by Weigl at 1-866-649-3445 or av2books@weigl.com with any questions, comments, or feedback.